KU-745-703

We've Got a Mission!

Designed by Carol Leslie & Nadeem Zaidi

Photo credits: Fluffy clouds © Craig Aurness/Corbis; Cirrus clouds © Randy Faris/Corbis; Cumulus clouds © W. Cody/Corbis; Cirrus clouds © W. Cody/Corbis; Cumulus clouds © Craig Aurness/Corbis; Storm cloud raining © Michael S. Yamashita/Corbis; Storm clouds and lightning © Bill Ross/Corbis; White clouds in blue sky © Craig Aurness/Corbis; White puffy clouds and blue sky © Brian A. Vikander/Corbis; Cumulus clouds seen from above © Royalty-Free/Corbis; Autumn leaves by rushing waterfall © Craig Tuttle/Corbis; Oak tree roots © Michael Boys/Corbis; Baobab tree © Wolfgang Kaehler/Corbis; Green hills © Bill Ross/Corbis; Green maple leaves © Ron Watts/Corbis; Rural New England farm in autumn © Darrell Gulin/Corbis; Watering can in low maintenance courtyard garden © Mark Bolton/Corbis; Purple corn cockle plants © Clay Perry/Corbis; Winter cress by water © Ian Rose/Frank Lane Picture Agency/Corbis; Blooming arrowleaf balsam roots © William Manning/Corbis; Wheatfield with Cypresses by Vincent van Gogh © National Gallery Collection; By kind permission of the Trustees of the National Gallery, London/Corbis; Michel Sardou – The Theatre of Paris © Richard Melloul/Sygma/Corbis; Hawke Bay, New Zealand © S. Borges/A. B./zefa/Corbis; Landscape, Crete Senesi, Tuscany, Italy © G. Rossenbach/zefa/Corbis; Beech tree and meadow, Spring © H. Spichtinger/zefa/Corbis; Landscape around the Lake Ebni, Germany © K. Hackenberg/zefa/Corbis; Egg © Royalty-Free/Corbis; Lakeside Grass and Mt. Hood © Craig Tuttle/Corbis; Blooming flowers around green cottage door © Richard Cummins/Corbis; Tree branch over running water © Photowood Inc./Corbis; Marshland on Martha's Vineyard © Peter Finger/Corbis; Person carrying guitar on beach © Anne Domdey/Corbis; Rocks in wash © Under the Light/Corbis; beach pebbles © Paul A. Souders/Corbis; Heart of shells in sands © Strauss/Curtis/Corbis; Sand dune at Cape Sebastian © Craig Tuttle/Corbis; Seashells on beach at Cape Hatteras © David Muench/Corbis; McClures Beach © Greg Probst/Corbis; Clam shells on the beach © George D. Lepp/Corbis; Seashell on beach © Paul Steel/Corbis; Starfish on kelp © Darrell Gulin/Corbis; Starfish on Maui Beach © Darrell Gulin/Corbis; Starfish on Maui Beach (2) © Darrell Gulin/Corbis; Conch shell on beach © Rose Hartman/Corbis; Picket fence on Huntington Beach © Zandria Muench Beraldo/Corbis; Red capped mushroom with spots © Kevin Schafer/Corbis; Monarch chrysalis © Paul Beard/Photodisc Green; Monarch forming chrysalis; © Paul Beard/Photodisc Green; Monarch forming chrysalis (2) © Paul Beard/Photodisc Green; Monarch forming chrysalis (3) © Paul Beard/Photodisc Green; Adult monarch © Paul Beard/Photodisc Green; Monarch Emerging From Chrysalis © Paul Beard/Photodisc Green; Monarch in Chrysalis © Paul Beard/Photodisc Green; Picture Frame © Burke/Triolo/Brand X Pictures; The River Slaney, County Wicklow, Ireland © Altrendo Travel; Water lilies and grasses in lake, Okavango Delta, Botswana © John Bracegirdle/Taxi; Fountain of Four Evangelists in central courtyard of San Juan Capistrano © Stephen Saks/Lonely Planet Images; Monomoy Point Lighthouse on South Monomoy Island, Cape Cod, Massachusetts © Michael Melford/National Geographic; Grand Teton National Park, Wyoming, USA, North America © Rob Mcleod/Robert Harding World Imagery; Bee (Poecilanthrax willistoni) on flower, close-up © Jim Cummins/Taxi; Side view of model of black and yellow bombardier beetle with yellow legs, cross section showing venom glands and reservoir, explosion chamber filled with red liquid with one-way valve, side view © Geoff Brightling/Dorling Kindersley; Close view of a grasshopper against a white background © Darlyne A. Murawski/National Geographic; Tropical Ants © Burke/Triolo/Brand X Pictures; Dragonfly © Burke/Triolo/Brand X Pictures; Fly © Digital Vision; Ladybug (coccinellidae) on blade of grass, close-up © Geostock/Photodisc Red;

Copyright © 2006 The Baby Einstein Company, LLC. All Rights Reserved. Little Einsteins logo is a trademark of The Baby Einstein Company, LLC. All Rights Reserved. EINSTEIN and ALBERT EINSTEIN are trademarks of The Hebrew University of Jerusalem. www.albert-einstein.org. All Rights Reserved.

Copyright © 2006 Disney Enterprises, Inc. All rights reserved.

ISBN 978-1-4054-9421-2

First published by Parragon in 2007
Parragon
Queen Street House
4 Queen Street
Bath BA1 1HE, UK

Butterfly
Suits

by Susan Ring
Illustrated by Katherine Nix & Kelly Peterson

Hey, Rocket is picking up some sounds on his Look-and-Listen Scope! Someone is singing a beautiful song in van Gogh's wheat fields. The Little Einsteins wonder just who is singing in the field below. Want to come along and find out? **GREAT! Let's go!**

Look! Do you see something on the red mushroom? It's the little guy that Rocket heard singing. Do you know what kind of animal he is? That's right, he's a caterpillar! In fact, he's a monarch butterfly caterpillar. They are yellow caterpillars with pretty stripes. What colour are his stripes? Have you ever seen a caterpillar before?

The Little Einsteins see a truck stop to pick up their friend. How many caterpillars do you see in the truck? Where do you think they are going?

Hmmm, Leo thinks the picture on the truck door might be a clue. What is it? Yes, it's a tree! And Annie thinks she knows where she's seen it before.

Wait a minute! I know that tree! It's the Musical Tree of Many Colours. That's the special place where caterpillars go to get brand-new outfits. How exciting!

Oh, dear! The truck hit a bump in the road. Poor little Caterpillar has fallen off the truck! Now how will he get to the Musical Tree of Many Colours? It will take Caterpillar an awfully long time to crawl to the tree. Hooray! Rocket has an idea. He sends a signal to Leo.

While on their way to the Musical Tree of Many Colours, Caterpillar got very, very hungry. Rocket found a nice spot on the beach where Caterpillar could enjoy a big pile of leaves. The team can't believe how much – and how quickly – Caterpillar is eating! They want to learn more about their new friend, so they ask Annie what she knows about caterpillars.

Caterpillar turned into a beautiful monarch butterfly. Have you ever seen orange-and-black butterflies like him flying in your neighbourhood?

When our friend was a caterpillar, he had a mouth and strong jaws that helped him quickly eat leaves.

Now that he's a butterfly, he doesn't have a mouth to bite into food with! Instead, he drinks flower nectar through a **proboscis,** which looks like a long, black tongue.

Can you find Butterfly's proboscis? When he isn't using it to sip nectar, his proboscis stays rolled up like a garden hose! Can you try to roll up your tongue? Only some people have that ability.